Introduction

"All good stewards save consistently, spend wisely, and give generously. The way we manage money affects the next generation." Robert Morris

This book is a series. If you have not read Tillie's Christmas Money, it is available at Amazon: Tillie's Christmas Money: Thompson, Tellia Ann: 9798551977100: Amazon.com: Books Reading the first book of the series will provide additional understanding of the story line. Each book delves into different concepts of the financial literacy process of the 3 S Money Rule: "Share, Save, Spend." For more information go to 3SMoneyRule.org.

Tillie's Birthday Money

It was early Friday morning and Tillie awakened very excited! She was thrilled that tomorrow would be her birthday. As Tillie stretched in her bed, she also remembered that it was Free Choice Fun Friday. Every Friday, her teacher, Mrs. Thompson always gave the students the opportunity to choose the website they wanted to visit to play games in their learning practice station. Tillie normally chose Khan Academy.

Just then, Tillie's alarm went off. Tillie jumped out of bed. She didn't want to be late getting to the bus stop. So she scurried to the bathroom to brush her teeth and wash up. As Tillie was getting dressed, she pondered how she was going to share the money she would get for her birthday. "There are so many good charitable organizations doing great things for the community," she thought. She wondered which one she would donate to.

"Why are you so excited and bubbly Tillie?" Justin moaned in a low, monotone, sarcastic voice after he finally dragged himself to the bus stop.

"I'm just excited because tomorrow is my birthday!" exclaimed Tillie.

"Oh, wow," he said. "You will probably get money. If you do, what will you use your birthday money for?" asked Justin.

"I'm not exactly sure," Tillie responded. "Um wait, I do know that I'm going to share some, save some, and spend some," Tillie answered.

"Yea, I remember when you got your Christmas money. You were going to spend that entire 50 bucks on bubble gum!" Justin said as he slapped his knee and laughed!

"That's crazy, right?" Tillie asked. "I can't believe I was going to spend all of that money on bubble gum. Although, I really do like bubble gum, I really do need bubble gum, I really got to have bubble gum!" Tillie said with a laugh.
"No way...we're not going to go through that again, are we?" Justin exasperatedly asked.
"I know, I know," said Tillie. "I was just messing with ya," she said. They both let out a big chuckle!

"Well, I'm not about to let that happen again," laughed Tillie. Just then the bus pulled up. Tillie and Justin got on the bus and sat next to each other.

Mrs. Thompson was standing at the door to greet her students and to remind them to get some hand sanitizer. As Tillie entered her classroom, she took the hand sanitizer and rubbed it in her hands until it was all dry. About that time, Krissy entered the room and she got some hand sanitizer as well.

"Hey Kris," said Tillie, greeting her friend.

"Hey Tillie, what's up?" Kris responded.

"What's up? What's up? What's up? It's my birthday tomorrow," Tillie exclaimed!

"I know, I know!" giggled Krissy. " I was up all night trying to figure out what to get you for your birthday."

"Oh, really?" Tillie asked while she rubbed her hands together in excitement.

"Yea, but you will have to wait until tomorrow to find out what I got you," Krissy said.

"Oh, can't you just give me a little hint? The anticipation is killing me softly and slowly," Tillie said while pretending to slowly fall on the floor.

"Well, you will just have to wait one more day," Krissy joked. Just then, the bell rang and the girls sat down in their seats.

"Good morning scholars!" their teacher said in a welcoming voice.

"Good morning Mrs. Thompson!" the students said in unison!

"Today, in Social Studies, we will be talking about goods and services and how money supports those services. Later on today in Math, we will review the different denominations and values money has. For example, a quarter is worth 25 cents, a dollar 100 cents, etc. So we will tie money values all together. Let's get started," Mrs. Thompson said.

Mrs. Thompson showed a video on goods and services. "Alright, this video explained the meaning of goods and services by showing examples. Since you have viewed the video, who can tell me how to get the goods or services? How do we obtain or get the things we need?" questioned Mrs. Thompson.

Lance raised his hand.

"I love that quiet hand raised Lance," Mrs. Thompson said with approval.   "Yes, you got it right Lance. We acquire the things we need traditionally in three ways. Now give me some examples," Mrs. Thompson said.

Lance began to give specific ways to use goods and services. "Well," Lance began, "Number 1, by someone donating or sharing them, like the book and book buddies that we got yesterday from that foundation.   Number 2 by saving the money that we earned from working and number 3 by spending our parents' money."

The whole class let out a big roar of laughter!

"Yes. I like to call it the 3 S Money Rule: SHARE, SAVE, SPEND. This is how we use money, by sharing some, saving some, and spending some. It is important to know that money is a tool that should be used when you need it and when you need it, you will have it!" Mrs. Thompson said.

"OMG, she must know my parents. That is the exact same thing they say," Tillie whispered to Tiffany. Mrs. Thompson continued. "I like that thought pattern Lance! You brilliant one! You gave us good examples of how people share. Does anyone else have any other examples of sharing? I'm thinking about when we were in the pandemic and how we saw a lot of organizations, social services, churches, sororities, fraternities, foundations, and individual people giving to help folks out during that difficult time. Okay, so shout it out," said Mrs. Thompson.

Danielle shouted, "My church gave away food." Several answers started to fly out of the students mouths. "Yeah, I heard the Urban League gave away food and toiletries," one student said.

"My aunt's sorority organized a clothing drive," another said.

"Oh that's right, my dad's company gave free internet services and hotspots," another shouted. "My grandmother's cafe made sandwiches to deliver lunch to families," someone else yelled out.

"Yes, yes, those are all fine examples of sharing," Mrs. Thompson said. "That is how people help their communities all over the world. I am so glad that we have families and a class that is kind, considerate, and believes in sharing."

"Secondly, let's talk about saving. So what does that mean? Can you save to get goods and services?" Mrs. Thompson asked. Krissy raised her hand. After being called on, she mentioned that last Christmas she saved some of the money she got from the last two Christmases to buy a hoverboard.

"I save 10% of the money I get for helping to watch my little brother," shouted Justin.

"Oh yeah, what are you saving for...to get a real haircut?" asked Lance. Once again the class roared to the top of their voices! "Ha, Ha, Ha you got jokes," laughed Justin!

"Alright, alright you geniuses, that's enough of that," Mrs. Thompson said smiling. Danielle raised her hand.

"I saved my Christmas money to get a bike, even though my Dad had to pitch in a little bit to help me," Danielle said proudly.

"Wonderful, so you all have a good handle on the concept of saving or a savings," Mrs. Thompson said.

"Lastly, let's go over spending," she said. "We know we have to spend money to get the goods and services we need and want."

"Mrs. Thompson?" Tillie interrupted, " you talked about the difference between a need and a want. I wish I had heard this lesson before I thought I needed to buy all of that bubble gum!"

Mrs. Thompson chuckled.   "Yes, Tillie there is a big difference between something that we want and something that we have to have, which is called a need. For example, we need food, clothes and shelter. The money that we earn should be used very wisely and intentionally to purchase those things. That's why I always say money is a tool to be used when we need it. It's really a good thing that we have money when we need it. I call it a sunny day fund... because it's "Oh Happy Day" when we need something and we have the money to purchase it, lol.

I'm glad you did not spend all of your money on bubble gum last Christmas and decided to share some, save some, and then spend some of that money," she said.

"Yes, I'm glad I have parents that know the importance of the "3 S Money Rule," Tillie said. "Perfect, your parents are very wise," Mrs. Thompson agreed. "That's probably why they have such a brilliant daughter!" Mrs. Thompson said as she and Tillie both laughed heartily!

"Okay scholars, let's review and wrap it up," their teacher said, turning more serious. We acquire the things we need by sharing, saving, and spending. Which is what I call the 3 S Money Rule: SHARE, SAVE, SPEND. We identified donations as another term for sharing. You can share by giving to others. Like I said earlier, there are organizations out there that we can give to, that help people out in a time of crisis. For example, our local church, food banks, community organizations, sororities, fraternities, societies, corporations, and individual endowments. We can give to any of these organizations and they will make sure the right people get the help they need."

"Also, we can take the money that we earned or that someone gives to us for Christmas, or our birthday, graduation, or any special occasion and save it for a later date to purchase something that we really, really want or need. You know something boys and girls, you don't have to have a lot of money to begin saving. If you start getting into the habit of saving a portion of everything you get, it will be easier when you get older. It's really sunny when you have the money you need and it's a rainy feeling when you don't have the money you need when you need it," Mrs. Thompson said with a funny smirk.

"Lastly, we should spend our own money, and not our parents' money, by earning money through doing chores around the house or for our neighbors. We heard that Lance babysits. What are some of the household jobs you guys have? Shout it out:" she said.

"Washing dishes," someone said.

"Walking the dog," said another.

"Cleaning out the birdcage, and washing cars," someone said.

Others loudly shouted other jobs like taking out the trash, doing the laundry, game coding, having garage sales, and selling items online.

There were many great student responses.

"As you know, today is Free Choice Fun Friday," Mrs. Thompson said. The entire class threw up happy hands🙌! "However, before you are released to your stations, please fill out your exit ticket," she said. Mrs. Thompson had the classroom helper pass out their exit ticket:

Exit Ticket

What is the Definition of sharing?

A. Give away everything you have

B. Give a portion or percentage of your earnings or what you have to help others in need

C. None of the above

Define Savings?

A. To keep a portion of your earnings or a portion of the money someone gives you to be used for a later time when needed.

B. To hoard all of the money you get and bury it like a pirate.

C. A and B.

Choose the best answer for spending wisely?

A. To use all of the money you get on goods and services.

B. To use all of the money you earn and all of the money someone else earns right away as soon as you get it.

C. To take a portion of the money you received from others or the money you earned and make a conscious well-thought-out choice of what to purchase, and when to purchase it.

When the students went out for recess, Danielle asked Tillie if she thought she would get any money for her birthday. "Yes, I'm sure I will," Tillie answered, "My Uncle Thomas always gives all the kids in our family money for our birthdays."

"Well, how are you going to use it?" Danielle inquired. "I'm not exactly sure," Tillie said. "I was trying to find the organization that I wanted to give to, especially since so many people were hurt by the pandemic. That global crisis was really something. Some people lost their jobs, didn't have enough to eat, and couldn't keep a place to stay. I heard the food pantries' supplies were almost depleted," Tillie stated.

"Yeah, COVID 19 is why we were out of school," Danielle said. "I'm glad we're back now. I saw some kids doing some real creative things during the pandemic. I read where this one boy and his brother put a claw machine on the driveway and had people put money in a slot machine to buy toilet paper for those in need. Other kids were giving free violin concerts on their porch to raise money to give to families to buy food." Krissy chimed in.

Later that day at Tillie's house, Tiffany and Tillie were talking . "I wonder what I'm going to get from my parents for my birthday," Tillie said.

"I bet your mom will make a contribution to your 529 College Savings Plan," laughed Tiffany. "Yea, you know she is going to take care of business before she does anything, lol."

"Right, well I guess you should be glad you have folks that teach you about the value of money. You know Tillie, a lot of kids our age don't know anything about money," sighed Tiffany.

"Yeah, like its purpose is to have it when you need it and when you need it you'll have it. Oh yeah, and what about the 3 S Money Rule? That's right...Share some money, Save some money, and Spend some money wisely," the girls said at the same time.

Just then, Tillie heard her Mom's footsteps coming up the stairs.

"Mom! Mom! Guess what I learned at school today?" she asked.

"Hey sweetie," her Mom said. "Tell me what you learned today!"

"Well," said Tillie. "My teacher was telling us the same thing you and Dad tell us all the time about the 3 S Money Rule... any time we get money we should share some, save some and lastly spend only what we need to spend so we can have money 💰 when we need it...and when we need it, we will have it." Tillie shared.

"Oh, is that right?" said Tillie's Mom. "Wow! it sounds like you were a very good listener today.   Mrs. Thompson really sounds like a real smart cookie," her mom said as she winked at Tiffany!

Tillie didn't know that Mrs. Thompson learned all of that from her Mom's book, Tillie's Christmas Money.

The next day at Tillie's birthday party, she ran excitedly to Krissy!

"I got it, I got it!" exclaimed Tillie.

Krissy looked surprised as she asked, "You got what?"

"I know what charity I'm going to share my birthday money with!" said Tillie.

"Well, good!" Krissy said, "Because I couldn't figure out what to get you, so I got you a visa gift card and now you can share it with your charity if you want; and oh yeah, don't forget about what our Sunday School teacher said. We are the arms and the legs of God. God uses us to get things for people."[1]

Tillie was so excited that she finally knew what organization she was going to share her birthday money with.

She then remembered when she was in Sunday School and her teacher, Bro. Calvin was talking about giving. He said when you give to the less fortunate it's like giving with a heavenly cause and you in return will be rewarded. [2]

After the party, on Monday, Tillie was riding home on the school bus when she saw a sign advertising chocolate rolls. She excitedly decided to sell chocolate rolls to add to the portion of the money she would get for her birthday. If she sold a bag of chocolate rolls for $2 that would help fund her donation. So she decided to buy a '5 lb.' bag of chocolate rolls for $10, put ten chocolate rolls in each goodie bag and sell them for $2. She knew this would bring her a good profit.

So Tillie set off on Saturday morning going to her family and friends and asking them to purchase a bag of chocolate rolls. She sold 20 bags. Tillie was very excited now because she had more money to give to the charity that she wanted. She spent $1 on the goodie bags and $1 on ribbon to wrap them real pretty. Her total expense was $12 so her profit was $28. Therefore, she added the $28.00 to the $7.00 from the sharing of her birthday money, making it a total donation of $35.00 to her charity.

Also, her aunt who worked at a bank decided to donate to every kid living there a bank filled with chocolate roll candy so that they could be reminded to share and save while enjoying their candy!

Tillie felt really good about herself knowing she was helping children in her own local community. Tillie's heart grew a little bit bigger that day because she had the opportunity to be self-productive and a changemaker by giving to others who were a little less fortunate than herself. Suddenly, Tillie realized she was the hands and feet her Sunday School teacher was talking about.

The End

DEFINITIONS:

SAVE – Keep and store up (something, especially money) for future use.

SHARE – To give a portion of (something) to another or others.

SPEND – To use up or pay out: Expend

PANDEMIC – occurring over a wide geographic area (such as multiple countries or continents) and typically affecting a significant proportion of the population.

DONATIONS – the making of a gift especially to a CHARITY or public institution.

ACQUIRE – to come into possession or control of

PONDER – to think about: reflect on

EXPENDITURE – disbursement, expense: (sentence example) Income should exceed expenditures.

ALLOCATION – to set apart or earmark: Designate

PROFIT – a financial gain, the difference between the amount earned and the amount spent in buying something.

CHARITY – an organization set up to provide help and raise money for those in need.

Source: Oxford Languages Dictionary and Merriam-Webster online

10 JOBS KIDS CAN DO NOW!

1. GRASS CUTTING
2. DOG WALKING
3. PET SITTING
4. HAIR BRAIDING
5. APP DEVELOPING
6. CODING
7. CAR WASHING
8. SNOW SHOVELING
9. BABY SITTING
10. ILLUSTRATING

Note To Reader: Notice, all of these words end in "ing" which indicates that they are active words. Most of these jobs are something you can quickly/actively do with your own raw talent and/or with minimal training.

"Poverty is the absence of self-production." Dr. Bill Winston

Here's Tillie's Cost Analysis:

5 lb Bag of Chocolate Rolls - $10.00

Bags	-	1.00
Ribbon	-	1.00
		_____
Total Expenditure		$12.00

20 Candy Bags sold at $2 per bag - $40

40-12 = $28 Total Profit

TOTAL ALLOCATION OF FUNDS

$50 from Uncle Thomas + $20 gift card = $70 for Tillie's Birthday Money

$7.00 (10%) = for Sharing

$7.00 (10%) = for Saving = $14.00

 Leaving Tillie $56 for Spending

Here's the breakdown: $70 - 7.00 - 7.00 = $56

IF YOU ENJOYED THIS BOOK, PLEASE LEAVE A REVIEW ON AMAZON
IT WILL ONLY TAKE A QUICK MINUTE. THANK YOU SO MUCH!

About the Author

T. A. Thompson is married to Calvin Thompson, otherwise known as Coach Cal. They have three financially successful adult daughters. T. A. is an educator, content creator and speaker. Although her educational background is reading literacy, her passion also includes financial literacy. She has always been intrigued about money matters and how money flows and investments. T. A. has fond memories of her grandmother keeping coins in her flowered handkerchief. She would often say ladies should always keep a little something saved. Her grandmother would say, "It's better to have when you need and when you need you have."

Upon attending a financial conference in 2010, Mrs. Thompson heard that the net worth of an African American woman was about $50. The speaker went on to say it's because they spend most of their disposable income on things. T. A. thought wow, we need to know how to acquire assets whether it be current, fixed, or etc. After returning to her Pre-K classroom on that Monday, her 4 year old student asked, "Mrs. Thompson, is that a Gucci purse?" Mrs. Thompson said yes and asked her if she knew what a piggy bank was for? The little girl said no. After that interaction with her Pre-K student, she felt compelled to get the message of financial intelligence to every young girl she could. She decided to inform young girls that they can save more and spend less money on things by making intelligent financial choices. From that day, T. A. became passionate to help change those stats through financial literacy especially for girls of color. Her principles are built on empowerment, education, and community service.

Mrs. Thompson holds a Bachelor's degree in Human Resource Management and a Master's in Education. She and her husband have owned and operated several businesses such as real estate, ground transportation, and trading the forex market. Throughout the years, she has shared her financial strategies and beliefs with her daughters, community, and urban schools. She created Financially Intelligent Girls Society (FIGS), to help mothers empower their daughters to make wise money choices. You can find financial tips for girls on her YouTube Channel: Financially Intelligent Girl https://www.youtube.com/channel/UClq9Xb6lic-sM_8n-YNIkEQ and her website 3 S Money Rule at: 3S moneyrule.org